Essential Oils for Witchcraft, Magic and Spells

by Sandra Willis

Table of Contents

1. Introduction

Essential oils are one of the most important (and also most overlooked) aspects of modern witchcraft. These oils have been crafted for hundreds or thousands of years, but their components are largely similar as their ancient counterparts. This means that using true essential oils in your spells is not only helpful - it's necessary. Altering the original recipes in the wrong way can have devastating effects on your craft, and may even compromise the final results.

There is such a wide variety of oils and other spell-casting products on the market, it can be difficult to determine which is the right choice for your needs - as well as how to properly utilize its power.

Each ceremony or ritual will have its own method of action, and this method will depend on your experience level, your materials used, and your dedication. Some of these rituals are symbolic, and do not hold any power in themselves, but refer to a time in our lives when we have grown power on our own.

More often than not, the rituals will call for specific items and tools - whether they are oils, or candles, or herbs - and it's important that you select the right materials for the job. Just as you wouldn't build a house out of butter, you shouldn't perform an incantation with the wrong materials, either.

Whether your ritual is specifically magic in nature or not, each separate tool has its own symbolism that can either enhance your result or turn the whole thing into a disaster. Spiritual oils are often considered the hidden fifth element that helps us reach out into the unknown and call upon the forces within us - whether we wish to communicate or produce a specific result.

Claim Your FREE Books at:

www.essentialoilsbookclub.com

2. Types of Oils

Most witches are aware of the multiple types of oils that are used in rituals and spells. There is a wide variety to cater to every need - but they are generally categorized as one of a few "types" of oils.

Each type of oil serves its own unique purpose, and not all are appropriate for magical applications. A fragrance oil, for example, being very different from an essential oil, will not fill the same purpose. It's best if you know the difference between your oil types in order to make sure you're using them for their intended purpose.

For as long as there has been magic, these different oils have been used in rituals and ceremonies - thousands of years of use, in some cases. Many of these oils are still on the market today, so we are still able to recreate these original spells and use them.

Ritual Oils

"Ritual oils" is a very general term describing the oils used to anoint tools, candles, and other such objects. These oils may also be used on the body as "anointing oils" (as often they have uses in both situations). Their power is limited, which is why they are typically combined with other ritual practices.

Condition Oils

We only really hear of "condition oils" when thinking of hoodoo spells and conjuring. This particular term refers to oils used in rituals and rites intended to immediately deal with some issue - whether a bad condition we wish to pass or a good condition we wish to find. They are also called Conjure Oils, Hoodoo Oils, and Lucky Oils because of their association with such magical practices.

Aromatherapy Oils

Aromatherapy dates all the way back to ancient civilizations, with historical proof of its practice in Egypt, Greece, Rome, and possibly China. It was shown to have cosmetic and curative benefits when these ancestors would burn scented flowers and herbs, as well as taking aromatic baths and massages using the extracted oils. This is still one of the most prevalent uses of magic today.

Fragrance Oils

In some instances, fragrance oils can be used in place of aromatherapy oils, depending on the goal you wish to achieve. Generally speaking, the magical essence of the source plant is not present in a fragrance oil, but they can be produced much quicker and cheaper than true essential oils. Whenever possible, it's best if you use true oils instead of artificially manufactured ones.

Essential Oils

"Essential oils" is another generalized term that refers to oils obtained by processing the source plant. These oils will characteristically taste or smell like their source materials. Used alone, they are best suited to fragrances, flavorings, and accents, but when properly combined they can harness the full potential power of the oils you use.

Handcrafted Oils

This term refers to oils that were created for a specific magical purpose. Whereas some witches choose to combine essential oils in order to use the power within, handcrafted oils are blended together from the start, and the bond between the source material will be stronger. They must be individually prepared and are not able to be factory produced, as each will have to be specifically formulated for the user.

Carrier Oils

Carrier oils are the only oils on this list that are specifically designed to not have magic within them. Carrier oils "dilute" stronger oils which may otherwise be too potent for use on the skin or in the air. In some uses, you may decide to use a hydrosol instead of diluting the oils in a carrier oil, but this is a matter of personal preference as well as specific spell.

3. The 5 Most Important Oils to Have

While your essential oil collection will be different depending on your specific needs, there are certain oils that should be kept in every witch's cabinet as they will be the ones you use most often. Each of these oils has its own distinct quality to be used for your benefit.

On your first trip to stock up your cabinet, you should make sure to grab at least one or two of each of these - and make sure you replace them when you start getting low. Where some oils may be substituted for one another, these five oils are generally the most common:

Lemon Oil
Lavender Oil
Tea Tree Oil
Eucalyptus Oil
Peppermint Oil

Lemon Oil

Lemon oil, in addition to its functions in certain spells, can aid as a degreaser and a household cleaner. It also adds an energizing scent to the home when used in aromatherapy rituals. It can be used in hand soaps, dishwater, and even to gently clean switch covers.

Lavender Oil

Lavender features proven calming effects, with the ability to soothe anxiety as well. It is commonly used in natural nerve-calming remedies for humans, babies, and pets alike, and it can even be used in a skin cream to help soothe and nourish. It's mild and gentle enough that it won't pose any risks to your pets and your children when used appropriately.

Tea Tree Oil

Tea tree oil is a natural sanitizer, which infinitely multiplies your uses for it in your pantry. This particular oil destroys the germs in your rituals and offers some protective capabilities. It can also be used as a topical ointment to repel infection and/or dark spirits.

Eucalyptus Oil

Eucalyptus oil is one of our personal favorites, as it not only helps as a cleanser, but it also has proven benefits within the respiratory system, as well as in spells which call for a boost to the user's prosperity and good fortune. Two drops in a mop bucket will help to ensure blessings and keep negative spirits at bay. Use on children's toys and furniture to kill germs and improve the immune system.

Peppermint Oil

Peppermint oil provides a powerful antibacterial, an anti-inflammatory medical treatment, and it helps to provide a cool, fresh feeling to the user. It can be used to help battle colds, stiff joints, hot flashes, and certain infections.

4. Aromatherapy

Aromatherapy, while often considered a form of magic, is not truly magical at its core - and as such is the only practice that can be substituted with fragrance oils instead of natural oils (as long as you are not hoping for magical results).

Aromatherapy has proven success with altering moods, minor health conditions, and even their mental capacities. The practice won't make you smarter, but it may help you unlock some intelligence you'd pushed aside. Some oils used in aromatherapy have even shown anti-microbial effects, speaking to their ability to heal.

Even though aromatherapy isn't magic, it's helpful to know what types of oils can be used for both purposes, as this will be a great benefit to you - spells that are more successful because they aren't just relying on one type of science.

There are, understandably, different types of oils to use for aromatherapy, as well, and knowing the difference between these can make all the difference.

Absolutes

The term "absolutes" refers to a fragrant type of oil that is extracted primarily from flowers. In order to obtain this type of oil, the delicate plant tissues (such as flower petals) are processed in a solvent or a fluid extraction. This method of extraction is particularly useful with plants that are too delicate for steam distillation or pressing. Some examples include tuberose absolute, beeswax absolute, and jasmine absolute.

Because of the use of solvents with the extraction process, some may remain within the oil after the extraction. For this reason, not all absolutes are suitable for use in potions that will be ingested or inhaled. You should always exercise extra caution when creating these types of potions as you may subject your user to toxicity if you don't know what you're doing.

Carrier Oils

Carrier oils are plant-based oils that are used to dilute essential oils or other herbal ingredients. These oils reduce the potency of the potion's other ingredients and make it safer to use on the skin. In some cases, carrier oils may be used to dilute ingredients that will be ingested, but usually oral methods will call for water dilution. Sweet almond oil is a very common carrier oil.

Essential Oils

Essential oils are a group of fragrant oils that are extracted with steam or by pressing. These oils, when sourced from natural plant materials, carry over some of the magical properties of the plants themselves. Most recipes that call for herbal ingredients can utilize pure essential oils just as well.

Hydrosols

The term "hydrosol" (or herbal distillate) refers to the part of the plant that is left behind in the water after an essential oil has been distilled. As this is essentially a by-product of essential oil production, in some cases (where the magical essence is centered in different parts of the plant) a hydrosol may have different functions than its essential oil or herbal counterpart.

Infusions

While the idea of an infusion is similar to the idea of a hydrosol, their applications are different. These infusions are simply plant material allowed to spread its essence in the water - as opposed to a byproduct of processing. Infusions often offer a milder version of the true herbal benefits of a plant (which will include the hydrosol effect as well as the essential oil effect). Chamomile is a very simple infusion for beginners.

Some Notes

You must know your user when you are creating any bioactive spell material. Essential oils may not be a safe measure for pregnant or lactating females (depending on the essential oil and the species of its user). In some cases, ingestion or topical application of certain oils may interact with conventional medications, as well as the potential for spells to directly interact if they are not compatible.

Since essential oils and absolutes are highly concentrated, carrier oils should be used for topical application to prevent skin irritation. We also recommend diluting with distilled water if your user will be ingesting a large amount of essential oils, as there is a potential to cause digestive complications with certain materials.

5. Special Types of Oils

Anointing Oils

Anointing oils are, most commonly, involved with the preparation of Rootwork or Hoodoo spells. These herbal-based combinations have been trusted by many generations of Hoodoo witches. We will not be sharing the recipes for these particular oils, but your trusted Hoodoo elders may be able to help you.

Cast Off Evil Oil

This particular oil is used to help rid the user of unwanted negative influences - whether false friends, bad habits, or discourse in the home.

Crown Of Success Oil

This oil is formulated to help its user to achieve success and recognition in all they do. This traditional oil helps to uplift your endeavors and guarantee your efforts will pay off.

Healing Oil

Traditionally, healing oil is used to help relieve your typical ailments - whether physical, emotional, or spiritual. It has the most effect with ongoing problems as opposed to sudden concerns.

Master Key Oil

If the user needs to quickly obtain knowledge or discipline in one particular area, the Master Key Oil helps to unlock the recesses of the mind to harness this inner power. It is also helpful when one wishes to gain authority and following - whether in the magical realm or the mundane.

Money Drawing Oil

The Money Drawing Oil is one of the oldest traditional Hoodoo oils that is still in use today. Fancied by bankers, business owners, gamblers, and workers alike, it is renowned for its ability to bring good fortune to its users.

Black Cat Oil

While many modern traditions consider black cats to be bad omens, Hoodoo culture calls upon the black cat as a symbol of strength and luck - especially useful when gambling and sporting. This older oil is common among those who engage in games of chance, but it can also help to reverse the effects of bad luck charms.

Fast Luck Oil

One of the most called-upon Hoodoo oils, Fast Luck Oil is commonly used to draw success in love, business, and chance. It also acts much faster than similar oils - it is the only oil to choose if you need results quickly.

Wick Oil

This particular oil has gone by many names, and it's not entirely certain which name is the "original" name and which are just copies. (It has been called Candle Oil, Brown Oil, Wick Oil, and even Special Oil #20 - although it is essentially an all-purpose condition oil, simply applied to candles.) Older conjurers claim that this came from a root-worker's recipe book, and the name Special Oil #20 referred to its placement as his 20th (and strongest) formula.

Van Van Oil

This is one of the most easily-recognizable oils in the Hoodoo arsenal, at point in history it was impossible to walk through New Orleans without smelling the distinct scent of Van Van Oil. It is most suited to dressing charms, anointing amulets, and blessing mojo bags. It is said to thwart negativity, refocus luck, and open the door to new opportunities.

6. Carrier Oils

Unlike the other types of oils on our list, carrier oils have no magical power. There is no power to be invoked, and there is no result to be obtained - they are simply used to help dilute the "active" oils in a particular recipe.

The decision of which carrier oils to use is largely a matter of personal preference because by definition they will not change the outcome of the spell. In some cases, you can use a magical oil as your carrier oil, but only for oils that are mild and complementary with your primary focus oil.

Following are some of the most commonly used carrier oils that you can easily find.

Almond Oil

Almond oil is a popular choice because the oil is easily absorbed into the skin. It has a very faint scent, which blends well into the scents of the oils you may be adding to it. It contains Vitamin D to help with non-magical benefits such as a hair treatment, dry skin serum, and a brittle nail fixer. It has a very smooth consistency and holds up well on a shelf. It may act as an allergen for some users with an almond allergy; this may be alleviated by using skin-free almond oil, but it may be best to choose a different carrier oil just to be safe.

Apricot Kernel Oil

Apricot kernel oil shares many of the properties of almond oil in its benefits, including applications on dry (or aging) skin. When used as a carrier oil, it infuses a light concentration of Vitamin A and a lighter consistency for topically-applied potions.

Avocado Oil

Avocado oil is a little heavier than some people may be comfortable with, but it is markedly richer in nutrients, and very gentle on sensitive skin. When the potion will be made into a skin serum, avocado oil guarantees improvement with dry skin.

Evening Primrose Oil

This carrier oil is a good choice for those with skin conditions such as eczema or psoriasis, as it can help to alleviate the physical symptoms of these conditions. Unfortunately, it has a significantly shorter shelf life than our other recommendations, averaging about two months before spoiling.

Grapeseed Oil

Grapeseed oil is well-known as a carrier to help with oily hair and skin. This is, in part, because of its light weight - it won't weigh your spells down as much as some of the heavier oils. It's also one of the least expensive carrier oils widely available.

Hazelnut Oil

If your goal is deep skin penetration, hazelnut is the carrier oil of choice. This oil deeply hydrates and nourishes because it is able to penetrate more quickly than many other oils. It has a potential to act as an allergen if the user is allergic to tree nuts. For these individuals, it is recommended you use a different carrier oil.

Jojoba Oil

Jojoba oil is commonly used in the treatment of acne and dandruff, as it applies just the right amount of moisture, combined with Vitamin E to promote healing. It is one of the lighter carrier oils as well, which allows it to dilute much easier.

Olive Oil

Olive oil is the most widely available oil that is appropriate to use as a carrier, being present in most grocery stores around the world. It does have a strong smell and may overpower the scent of the "active" oils, which can be beneficial if the user isn't fond of the source material scents.

Peach Kernel Oil

This oil is wonderful for use on the face, as it contains a plentiful amount of Vitamins A and E. It is also light which may be preferred.

Soya Oil

Soya oil is very rich in Vitamin E and is easily absorbed by most users. It is pet-safe and readily available. However, a small portion of users with a soy allergy may have an allergic reaction to soya oil. Most with a soy allergy can topically use the oil with no issues, but it's recommended you test a small, out-of-sight contact point before prolonged use.

Sunflower Oil

Sunflower oil is wonderful for those seeking a higher nutritional benefit to their oil (as it is high in both Vitamin E as well as essential fatty acids). However, you should be advised that it does have a stronger scent; This may be beneficial for a user who isn't drawn to the scent of their blend.

Wheat Germ Oil

Wheat germ oil is of particular benefit to those with aging skin, as it contains Vitamins A, B, C, and E. It helps to tone and firm, reduce the appearance of stretch marks and scars, and can even help to minimize facial blemishes. It has a stronger scent than many essential oils, which can be a benefit to those who don't enjoy the scent of their potion.

7. Planetary Oils

The respective oils for each planetary power are used to draw upon the essence of that particular god or goddess, and they help to invoke the characteristics when used in conjunction with experienced magic. Common practices include candle anointing as well as personal scents. These oils will help to reveal the power of the planets they correspond with. Some also correspond with a particular day of the week.

If you are in need of a particular astrologically-based spell, these oils can be combined with the corresponding zodiacal oil to intensify and vitalize. If you are interested in learning the recipes for these oils, please speak with your trusted elders.

Sun Oil

Also referred to as Sol or Apollo. This oil corresponds with the ruling of Leo. Power over Sunday.

Mercury Oil

Also referred to as Hermes or Wotan. This oil corresponds with the ruling of Gemini and Virgo. Power over Wednesday.

Venus Oil

Also referred to as Freya This oil corresponds with the ruling of Taurus and Libra. Power over Friday.

Earth Oil

Also referred to as Terra or Gaia. This oil corresponds with the ruling of mother nature.

Moon Oil

Also referred to as Luna or Artemis. This oil corresponds with the ruling of Cancer. Power over Monday.

Mars Oil

Also referred to as Twi. This oil corresponds with the ruling of Aries; co-ruling of Scorpio, along with Pluto (Hades).

Jupiter Oil

Also referred to as Zeus or Thor. This oil corresponds with the ruling of Sagittarius; co-ruling of Pisces, along with Neptune (Poseidon). Power over Thursday.

Saturn Oil

Also referred to as Kronos. This oil corresponds with the ruling of Capricorn; co-ruling of Aquarius, along with Uranus (Urania). Power over Saturday.

Uranus Oil

Also referred to as Urania. This oil corresponds with the co-ruling of Aquarius, along with Saturn (Kronos).

Neptune Oil

Also referred to as Poseidon. This oil corresponds with the co-ruling of Pisces, along with Jupiter (Zeus, Thor).

Pluto Oil

Also referred to as Hades. This oil corresponds with the co-ruling of Scorpio, along with Mars.

8. Zodiacal Oils

Zodiacal oils are formulated in respect to the zodiac. They help to bring out the zodiacal traits of each sign and to amplify the symbolism between them. These oils may be used in conjunction with candle magic, or combined with Planetary Oils to create a tropical scent. This combination will help to strengthen the areas of your astrological persona that are lacking, or to help heighten the stronger characteristics.

Please consult the following list to determine the oils that are best suited to your needs.

The Oils for Fire Signs

Aries, or the Ram. In power from March 21 - April 21 and ruled by the planet Mars.

Leo, or the Lion. In power from July 21 - August 21 and ruled by the sun.

Sagittarius, or the Archer. In power from November 21 - December 21 and ruled by the planet Jupiter.

The Oils for Earth Signs

Taurus, or the Bull. In power from April 21 - May 21 and ruled by the planet Venus.

Virgo, or the Virgin. In power from August 21 - September 21 and ruled by the planet Mercury.

Capricorn, or the Sea Goat. In power from December 21- January 21 and ruled by the planet Saturn.

The Oils for Air Signs

Gemini, or the Twins. In power from May 21 - June 21and ruled by the planet Mercury.

Libra, or the Balance. In power from September 21 - October 21 and ruled by the planet Venus.
Aquarius, or the Water Bearer. In power from January 21 - February 21 and ruled by the planets Uranus and Saturn.

The Oils for Water Signs

Cancer, or the Crab. In power from June 21 - July 21 and ruled by the moon.
Scorpio, or the Scorpion. In power from October 21 - November 21 and ruled by the planets, Pluto and Mars.

Pisces, or the Fishes. In power from February 21 - March 21 and ruled by the planets, Neptune and Jupiter.

9. Essential and Fragrance Oils

Essential oils, when used in the correct combinations, can be truly magical. We have compiled a few of the most common oils that can be used with a carrier oil.

Also, please note that fragrance oils and essential oils are not the same thing. Fragrance oils, when suspended in carrier oils, can be used as a personal scent, but should not be used in spells because their composition is different than the essential oil that is intended. When at all possible, you should ensure that you are only using high-quality essential oils from natural source materials.

Basil Essential Oil

Basil oil helps to relieve mental and intellectual fatigue. This has a positive effect on the mood and encourages enthusiasm for the task at hand. It aids with memory, concentration, and positive thinking. It is considered the "rejuvenation" oil.

Bergamot Essential Oil

Bergamot oil helps with anxiety, stress, and tension when the user is mentally drained. This promotes a sense of internal balance and helps to encourage the user to continue pursuing their goal. It is considered the "motivation" oil.

Calamus Essential Oil

Calamus Oil deals directly with charisma and natural talents, and is best suited to endeavors that require the user gain mastery in a short time. It can also be used to help attain control of a difficult situation. This is considered the "leadership" oil.

Cedarwood Essential Oil

Cedarwood helps to promote a stable frame of mind, as well as eliminating mental strain. This is directly associated with relaxation and helps to bring a sense of calm. It is considered the "clarity" oil.

Chamomile Essential Oil

Chamomile is widely known to soothe both the mind and the body to attain ultimate relaxation. It helps with all manners of stressful situations, such as asthma, migraines, tension, anxiety, and everyday stress. It is known as the "soothing" oil.

Coriander Essential Oil

When your user needs to be assured that stress and fatigue will stay at bay, coriander helps to harness every drop of motivation and skill in order to create a sense of calm. It gives the user confidence to tackle the task at hand with ease, and is often considered an "optimism" oil.

Eucalyptus Essential Oil

Eucalyptus shows benefits to the mind and the body, and it helps the user to reach a relaxed, peaceful state. It helps with infections (including the common cold), it prevents discomfort, and it calms a busy mind. It is widely considered the "focus" oil.

Fennel Essential Oil

Fennel oil helps to regulate mental blockages to prevent mental exhaustion and overwhelming situations. It helps to smooth the flow of the thought process in order to allow the user to stay more motivated. It is considered to be a "preparation" oil.

Helichrysum Essential Oil

Helichrysum oil offers a wonderful combination of illness-fighting properties and tension-busting power. It has applications in stress relief and tension reduction. It helps to prevent the discomfort of infections such as colds and flu by fighting the problem at the first sign rather than waiting for symptoms to show. It is considered the "health" oil.

Jasmine Fragrance Oil

In scent-dependent potions, jasmine fragrance oil is great to open your inner eye to its psychic potential. It can help when you are just starting in astral travel and similar clairvoyant endeavors. This is considered the "psychic" scent.

Lavender Essential Oil

Lavender oil is best suited to magical projects that involve health or love. It is also widely known to have a calming effect on both the physical and spiritual body and is often used as a mood enhancer. When used in rejuvenation spells, it helps to clear the senses to reduce frustration and stress. It is considered the "calming" oil.

Lotus Fragrance Oil

Lotus fragrance oil shows its best benefit when used in spells relating to love and spirit. It can also be used to help summon the Water dieties as well as the Moon. This is considered the "water" scent.

Mandarin Essential Oil

With the light citrusy scent, mandarin oil helps to relax the body, inside and out. It is a suitable companion to chamomile as well as lavender when you desire stronger calming results. It is considered the "helper" oil.

Patchouli Essential Oil

Patchouli is associated with money and protection, so it is best suited to workings that involve these areas of the user's life. However, it shows to be quite effective for matters of love and sex as well. In milder applications, it helps to relieve fatigue and prevent anxiety. It is widely considered the "protection" oil.

Other Essential Oils for Relaxation

You may have noticed that there are quite a few essential oils that deal directly with relaxation and stress, and this is no coincidence. In most instances of magical workings, there is a greater success rate for the user if they are able to believe that the treatment will work - and sometimes, all that's standing in the way is a little bit of doubt. Any of these relaxing oils can help to alleviate this doubt as well as promoting an all-around sense of calm.

If the particular scents of the relaxation oil your recipe calls for, you may choose to substitute with one of the following: Lemongrass, melissa, orange, peppermint, pine, tuberose, or ylang ylang. Be sure to consult with someone more experienced if there is a question whether their results are similar enough to make the switch. In some cases, you may need to combine "substituted" oils to get the same effect.

Claim Your FREE Books at:

www.essentialoilsbookclub.com

10. Oil-Based Potions

Depending on the oils and the specific potions, they may be a part of the spell crafting itself, a part of the spells casting, a minor rite, or a major rite.

It's necessary that you have dark potion bottles to keep your potions in - lighter bottles may let the light seep in and ruin the composition of your potion. They should be kept in a dark cabinet and tightly sealed once filled. If the lid is loose, the air may ruin the integrity of the potion (or it may leak).

All of your bottles should stay well-labeled. Each should include the name of the potion, the intention you have with it (including the intended user, if you are making potions for others), and the ingredients. For many potions, it may be beneficial to include the phase the moon was in when you made the potion, as some may be best saved for similar lunar conditions. Most blends will have a very limited life expectancy, so keeping the proper dates is imperative.

Essential oils must never be used on the skin unless they are properly prepared and diluted. It is advisable to do a skin patch test as well, just to ensure that there are no adverse reactions. Make sure you wash your hands after mixing your oils, as even those which do not cause a severe reaction may present some when left on for an extended period of time.

Overall, the most important thing to remember is that you should always exercise the utmost caution when dealing with essential oils and all magical workings in general. If you have any doubts about your abilities, please consult with an older, more experienced witch.

We have compiled some of the most commonly used spells that one might find useful in your day-to-day activities. This list in no way represents the full possibilities of essential oil magic, but it will give you a solid foundation to help you build your practice.

Essential Oil Blends You Can Use!

Altar Oil

4 tsp Frankincense Oil
2 tsp Myrrh Oil
1 tsp Cedarwood Oil
4 tsp carrier oil of your choice

Blend your oils together in a dark bottle while calling upon the deity (or deities) you wish to summon. This recipe calls for a full 13 cycles of the moon when stored appropriately. Anoint the altar at every full moon, and optionally at new moon as well. Keep tightly capped in a cool, dark place.

Anointing Oil #1

5 tsp Sandalwood Oil
3 tsp Cedarwood Oil
1 tsp Orange Oil
1 tsp Lemon Oil
4 tsp carrier oil of your choice

This can be used to anoint bodies before ritual practices, or to bring about blessings. This recipe is enough for approximately 12 uses, but you may be able to get more uses out of it if you use less.

Anointing Oil #2

2 tsp Patchouli Oil

2 tsp Cinnamon Oil
2 tsp Verbena Oil

If you are not trying to anoint human bodies for your ritual, you may choose to work with our secondary anointing oil instead. This oil has a strong scent and is wonderful for candle work. The recipe calls for one to two sessions, depending on the size of your candle room.
Starting from the center of the room and working toward the edges, cover the entire candle with oil, starting at the middle. Visualize the intent of your work today while you anoint the candles you will be using. For additional cleansing and purification of your sacred space, wipe your altar or ritual area as well. For more private sessions, you may choose to add this oil blend into the bath water before meditation.

Astral Travel Oil

5 tsp Sandalwood Oil
1 tsp Ylang Ylang Oil
1 tsp Cinnamon Oil

This blend helps to propel the user into the astral plane when used in conjunction with the appropriate rituals. It is best breathed in from a shallow dish during meditation.

Attraction Oil

1 tsp Lovage Herb
1 tsp Lemon Peel
1 tsp Rose Petals
1 tsp Lemon Balm
3 tsp Carrier oil of your choice

This mixture must be used for the three waxing days before the full moon. Start by mixing the herbs together. The herb mixture should be soaked in the oil, and the oil used to anoint a small piece of Lodestone. Set the anointed stone out under the night sky for three full days and nights, ensuring that the stone remains charged by the oil the entire time. (You may need to re-anoint the Lodestone in order to do this.)

Divination Oil

1 tsp Musk Oil
1 tsp Ambergris Oil
1 tsp Violet Oil
1 tsp Lilac Oil

Divination oil will not give will not give the power of divination to those who are not already skilled in it, but those who use this particular blend will see an increase in the clarity of their psychic visions and more clear eyesight. To use, blend all oils together in a dark glass bottle. Apply one drop each to the third eye and the temples. This will also help you to discern the meanings behind your visions.

Initiation Oil

3 tsp Frankincense oil
3 tsp Myrrh Oil
1 tsp Sandalwood Oil

Initiation oil works best when breathed in, and when formulated correctly can increase the user's perceptiveness to the spiritual realm. It is often used in mystic initiation ceremonies for the way it allows the user to communicate with the dead.

Prophetic Dreams

6 tsp carrier oil of your choice

3 tsp Jasmine Oil
1 tsp Rose Oil

This oil helps to guide your dreams into psychic or spiritual revelations by igniting your innermost senses. The blend works well when placed in an oil diffuser while the user is sleeping, or by topically applying the oil to the temples before bedtime.

Protection Oil #1

4 tsp Basil Oil
3 tsp Rose Geranium Oil
2 tsp Pine Oil
4 tsp Sesame Oil (or other carrier oil of choice)

This oil mixture should be made up in advance if possible, as the user may choose to wear oil-soaked herbs on his person in order to ward off negative spirits and danger. For those who choose not to use the herbs, you may choose to anoint windows, doorways, and other openings in order to keep bad energy out of the home.

Protection Oil #2

5 tsp Petitgrain Oil
5 tsp Black Pepper Oil -or- 4 tsp Basil Oil
3 tsp Geranium Oil
2 tsp Pine Oil

Wear this as a personal scent in order to defend against those who wish to bring you harm. This can also be used to anoint doors, windows, and other openings in order to protect the home from negative energy. Do not combine the two protection oils together, as their ingredients can cause unintended consequences when mixed.

Psychic Visions Oil

4 tsp Lemon Grass Oil
2 tsp Bay Leaf Oil
1 tsp Nutmeg Oil
3 tsp Hazelnut Oil (or other carrier oil of your choice)

Unlike the Divination Oil, this Psychic Visions Oil is specifically created to help extend psychic visions to those who are not particularly prone to them. When the forehead is anointed with this mixture, it can cause the user's psychic awareness to expand, which will manifest itself in dreams.

Purification Oil

4 tsp Frankincense Oil
3 tsp Myrrh Oil
1 tsp Sandalwood Oil

This oil helps to relieve its user of any negative energies and toxic thoughts that may be clinging to their person. Many witches prefer to mix this into bath water, as it provides a very relaxing scent. Others choose to mix it with 6 tsp of carrier oil (almond oil is a great choice) and wear it as a personal scent to eliminate negative energies.

CPSIA information can be obtained
at www.ICGtesting.com
Printed in the USA
LVHW080935310820
664580LV00016B/1625